THAT GOOD OLD BOY FROM ACWORTH, GA IS BACK

MORE STORIES OF GROWING UP IN ACWORTH IN THE FIFTIES AND LATER LIFE

Lou,
Hope you Enjoy my
True Stories.
God Bless!

Walter Flanagan

ISBN: 978-1-6847-1638-8 (sc)
ISBN: 978-1-6847-1637-1 (e)

Because of the dynamic nature of the Internet, any web addresses or links contained in this book may have changed since publication and may no longer be valid. The views expressed in this work are solely those of the author and do not necessarily reflect the views of the publisher, and the publisher hereby disclaims any responsibility for them.

Any people depicted in stock imagery provided by Getty Images are models, and such images are being used for illustrative purposes only. Certain stock imagery © Getty Images.

Lulu Publishing Services rev. date: 12/31/2019

DEDICATION

THANKS FOR THE MEMORIES

After I wrote my first book, 'Stories of A Good Old Boy From Acworth, GA, Growing Up in Acworth in the Fifties and Beyond', and had a book signing, I began to get messages from Facebook friends and others who had purchased the book thanking me for bringing back memories of growing up in Acworth, GA in the fifties.

One lady told me her twenty year old grandson was visiting and my book was on the coffee table. He picked it up and read the opening story wherein I recall in the fifties having telephone service and we were on a party line with two other families. If the phone rang one time or three times, you did not answer it. Our calls were identified by two rings. Sometimes, when you were ready to make a call, you picked up the receiver and someone else would be on the phone. You politely hung up and waited until they finished before you could make your call. She messaged me that he asked her, "Grandma, is this true about having telephones with a party line?" She said, "Sit back and let me tell you how it was." She told him about the dial telephones that were not portable like the cellphones of today. She also told him about pay phones that you could find when you were away from home and that you could deposit five cents and make a local call.

Another Facebook message thanked me for bringing back memories of going to the Legion Theater in Acworth in the 50s, the ten to fourteen cent admission and the smell of fresh popped popcorn which was five cents a bag. A fountain coke was also five cents. He told me his allowance was twenty-five cents per week, same as mine.

One lady I met on a subsequent trip to Acworth said she too missed the chimes from the church that played every evening just about sundown. We both wished we could hear those chimes play The Old Rugged Cross again. I mentioned to her the whistle at Unique Knitting Mill that you would hear at noon. She remembered it too.

These are only a few of the comments I received from those who had read my first book. Acworth is collecting pictures, newspaper articles and other things for the recently completed Acworth History Museum. I visited this facility and it was a great experience. I will go back every time I'm in Acworth. Thank you to all involved in this effort.

Thanks to my sister Wilma and others who urged me to write more stories about growing up in Acworth. With these stories in my second book, I hope to stir more memories of Acworth in the fifties. Enjoy!

CONTENTS

MY FIRST AND ONLY BICYCLE

In my first book, I described how my dad bought me a bicycle. It was scratched and he bought it on sale at the Western Auto next to the railroad crossing in Acworth. Since our family didn't have a car, my dad rode the bicycle home. It was a twenty-six inch bicycle and I couldn't wait to jump on it and take a ride. I rode down Fowler Street which was a dirt road at the time. There was a wash out across the road in front of the Ray Dean's home. I had a hard time sitting on the seat and reaching the pedals, so I stood on them. Unfortunately, when I hit the wash out, my feet slipped off the pedals and I landed my groin area on the cross bar. Ouch! I fell over, but the bicycle was not damaged.

My friend Bobby Odom who lived down Fowler Street had a bicycle and we explored Acworth Beach, downtown Acworth and anywhere we wanted to ride. Well, I got so much use from that bicycle, but, in the early sixties, when I went to work at the Atlanta Post Office, I had not ridden the bicycle in several years. One day I saw Ronnie Kennedy, our next door neighbor, and he didn't have a bicycle. He was about the age I was when my father bought the bike for me. I took some spray paint, painted the bike, and gave it to Ronnie. It was fun to see him riding that bicycle. Brought back memories of me riding it for the first time. Luckily, for Ronnie, Fowler Street was paved so he didn't have to look out for wash outs!

MISS HELEN HARTLEY

Miss Hartley was a teacher at Acworth School and, later, North Cobb High School. She was my sixth grade teacher in 1956 at Acworth School in the 'shack' located near the main buildings. The 'shack' was a detached wooden building located on one of the 'flats' at the school. She was a single lady and an excellent teacher.

She would give us a list of words and definitions early in the week and, on Fridays, we would have a test which would require correct spelling and definitions of the words. About every three weeks, we would split the class and, standing on different sides of the room, we would have a spelling bee. She would say the word, then we would repeat the word, render our spelling and hope it was correct. If it wasn't, we had to sit down. The object was to remain standing as long as you kept spelling the words correctly. I was usually one of the last five or six standing near the end of our competition.

She exposed us to so much I had never seen. After lunch, she would read to us for about fifteen minutes from books she chose. She also had several parents who volunteered to drive those who would go for field trips. I recall going to Atlanta to the Roxy Theater to see Cinerama. It was a movie filmed with three cameras and projected onto a center screen and two other screens, one on each side of the big screen. It gave you the illusion that you were there. One of the scary scenes was riding in the first car on a roller coaster. Before going to the theater, we ate lunch at the Ding Ho restaurant. I had never had Chinese food in my life until that day.

On another trip, she took us to the Monastery in Conyers, GA. We toured the grounds and attended a service inside after seeing the quarters of those who studied there. I remember the girls had to sit in the balcony and had to have a scarf over their heads. Another trip was to Ponce de Leon ball park to see the Atlanta Crackers baseball team. This was well before the Atlanta Braves came to Atlanta. I still remember Bob Montag was the star player. We had programs that evening and I so regret throwing mine in the trash after the game.

One day, we walked from the 'shack' to Center Street in Acworth, a distance of just over one quarter mile. The fire truck was pulled into the street and the firemen gave us a demonstration of using the hose on the truck to put out fires. We got to go up individually and hold on to the nozzle while water was spraying through the hose. Wow, what a thrill for this youngster. Another time, we walked to the Legion Theater in Acworth to see the movie Apache, starring Burt Lancaster. She tied that in to our reading about American Indians and the Trail of Tears as I recall.

Another time, we walked about one quarter mile down to Acworth Beach to enjoy an afternoon we won as a result of some contest, the details I cannot recall. I do remember it was the first time I was able to swim out to the raft. We enjoyed the swings and playing on the beach. We walked down to the beach on another occasion and, this time our assignment was to sit at one of the picnic tables looking out over the lake and draw a picture. I learned I was not an artist. Miss Hartley also worked at the beach on some weekends running the miniature golf course.

When North Cobb High School opened in 1958, it was my freshman year. I had Miss Hartley for my homeroom teacher. She also taught Latin. I did not take a Latin course as I was still struggling with English, especially diagramming sentences. I wonder if they still do that in school?

In 2010, at a North Cobb multi-year class reunion held at Pinetree Country Club, one of my classmates said he had seen Miss Hartley. He said she was living in Corbin, Ky and was still teaching. I asked for her address and he gave it to me. I wrote her a letter, sent her a picture, and told her about my career once I left North Cobb. She wrote me back and told me she was still teaching part-time telling me about the children of Appalachia.

In the last paragraph of that letter, she said she hoped I was still reading and, she gave me a reading assignment of a book about Appalachia, the hard times, and the children. In 2014, after I had my first book published, I sent her another letter and a copy of my book. Sadly, she did not respond to my letter. I pray all is well with this wonderful lady who exposed this good old boy from Acworth to so much in our sixth grade class in the 'shack'.

SCHOOL BOY CRUSH

Her name was Delight Harper, and she was a junior and I was in the eighth grade, a sub-freshman. She was a pretty lady who played trumpet in the Acworth High School Band. I was lucky enough to be seated beside her in the trumpet section. Delight helped me with my initiation into the Acworth School 'A' band from the Acworth School 'B' band. This is what we do when we play concerts, watch the director for dynamics, etc. When we marched, she reminded me to look from side to side and stay in formation, and taking eight steps to five yards when we marched on the football field.

I would see her occasionally in the hallway and she would always smile and say hello. I had a case of acne and not a lot of self-confidence when I was in the eighth grade, and here was a pretty junior class lady who smiled and spoke to me.

This is a short story, but it reveals how one nice lady made a lasting impression on me. She went out of her way to help a younger student adjust to a new surrounding in the Acworth High School Band. I recently learned she passed away a few years ago. RIP Delight, and I'll never forget your kindness to a bumpy faced boy in the eighth grade.

MR. WES BAXTER, BAND DIRECTOR

MR. WES BAXTER
Director

I played trumpet in the Acworth School Band and, when North Cobb High School opened, played in the band for all four high school years there. Wes Baxter was our Band Director at Acworth School and for a couple of years at North Cobb. He was an outgoing fun loving man who enjoyed his job.

I'll never forget one year when our football team played an away game. For some reason, our tuba player was unable to make the trip. Mr. Baxter donned a band uniform and played tuba. As we were lining up along the sideline about to march onto the field and perform our half time show, he was standing next to me. We were facing the field and a guy behind us said, "Hey fat boy, play us a song." Mr. Baxter turned to me and said, "He's talking to you." A few seconds later, the guy yelled again, "Hey fat boy with that big horn, play us a song." Mr. Baxter said nothing after that. It was then time to begin our half time show. He left North Cobb for my junior and senior years in band.

My next encounter with him was when my first wife and I went to dinner one Saturday evening with her parents at Lakeside Country Club in 1976. Mr. Baxter's dance band was playing at the club that evening. He and I talked for a few minutes while his band was on break and caught up with our lives since he left North Cobb. I told him I had taught myself to play drums in 1966, had played with a band on weekends for about six years, and was currently playing with the Swinging Gentlemen from WPLO. I was also a Labor Relations Representative at the Atlanta Post Office and was attending Georgia State College two nights per week. Mr. Baxter told me after he left North Cobb, he attended law school and, after passing the bar exam, he opened his law office in Smyrna, GA. We congratulated each other on our accomplishments and it was back to the stage for him.

The last time I saw him was at a North Cobb High School multi-year reunion several years later. I told him that, prior to this reunion, I had looked through my high school yearbooks and appreciated his written comments in my yearbook in his last year at North Cobb. He said he still had his law office in Smyrna. A good man who taught me so much about music. Thank you Mr. Baxter.

Walter: You have been a real "hoss" in our NCHS Trumpet section. Without you the Football band would have been mighty weak. Thanks for your loyalty, cooperation and determination. I wish you the very best in everything.

Sincerely,

Wes Bayder

We, the Senior Class of North Cobb High School in appreciation for his outstanding work in the music department, dedicate the 1960 Panorama to

Mr. Wes Barton

ACWORTH GOLF ASSOCIATION

I began playing golf in 1957 after seeing it on television. I bought my set of J. C. Higgins golf clubs at the Sears & Roebuck in Marietta for $39.95. The set was a golf bag, a 1 and 3 wood, a 3, 5, 7 and 9 iron and a putter. With this set, I taught myself to play. I practiced my short game on the two acres across from our Fowler Street home. Mr. Banks, a Fowler Street neighbor, worked with me on my grip and swing. Bill Towe, a customer at Dunn's Supermarket where I worked on weekends, had his golf clubs in his car and, one Saturday when I placed groceries in his car and noticed his clubs, we began talking about golf. He asked if I wanted to go to Rockmart with him and play golf Sunday morning. Absolutely, and that began a friendship with golf every Sunday at the Goodyear Golf Course in Rockmart, GA. Later, when O. B. Keeler Golf Course opened in Kennesaw, we played our Sunday rounds there as it was a public course when it opened.

The first time I recall hearing about the Acworth Golf Association was in the late 50s while I was waiting to get a haircut at Chandler's Barber Shop on Main Street in Acworth. Aubrey Chandler was talking to another golfer and he said the Association was talking with Cobb County government about the possibility of building a golf course across the lake from Acworth Beach. On our next Sunday golf outing, I relayed this information to Bill who was an electrician working for the City of Acworth.

Bill checked into the Association and found they sponsored tournaments throughout the year. He said we should join, so we did. I think it was ten dollars a year membership fees. I can't recall the names of all the members, but I do remember some. Aubrey Chandler, Grady Gee, Bill Brown, Kenneth Hufstetler, Little Boy Scroggs, Coach Sewell, Bill Towe and me. One of our tournaments at the nine hole Goodyear Golf Course in Rockmart brings back memories. Bill and I were in a foursome with Little Boy Scroggs and another golfer. On a par 5 hole with a wide fairway, Little Boy, a really good baseball player, killed a drive down the middle of the fairway. After hitting the ball, he uttered a couple of profanities. Bill said, "What's wrong Little Boy?" He replied, with a slight grin on his face, "I broke my damn tee." I turned away so he wouldn't see me laugh.

When Cobb County opened the O. B. Keller Golf Course in Kennesaw, they had a match featuring Sam Snead and Tommy Aaron playing Arnold Palmer and Coby Ware. Bill and I attended this event and, near the clubhouse, in a wheelchair, was Bobby Jones. The featured golfers and many in the crowd talked with him, and I've wished so many times that I would have gotten some autographs. We followed the four golfers round the course as they played their match, but I can't recall who won.

In 1962, I won a trophy in an Acworth Golf Association tournament at O. B. Keeler Golf Course. I won the third flight, and took my trophy to Lanier Jewelry in Acworth for engraving. It was the first trophy I ever won and I was so proud of it. It still sits on a shelf in my home with a few other trophies from my golf and tennis participation.

Several years ago, a golf course was constructed on the land across the lake from Acworth Beach. I played it after it had been open a year or so and, as I looked out over the lake, I wondered how many of those in the Acworth Golf Association had lived to play the course.

COACH SEWELL WANTS ME TO PLAY FOOTBALL

DADDY, COACH SEWELL WANTS ME TO PLAY FOOTBALL

Mr. Emory Sewell

I t was 1958 and our first year at North Cobb High School. The school was located approximately half way between Acworth and Kennesaw. Those of us from Acworth who had gone through the first eight years at Acworth School met many new friends from Kennesaw.

The first year at North Cobb, our football field was not ready for play so the games were played at Coats & Clark field in Acworth. Our physical education (PE) classes were used to pick up rocks off the North Cobb football field. We used wheelbarrows to cart the rocks off the field. We would get in some occasional games along with the work, but one day in September 1958 I will always remember.

Coach Emory Sewell was our PE teacher, so, on this particular day, we were going to compete in a fifty yard dash. Our runs would be timed. I was six feet, one inch tall and weighed approximately 215 pounds. After my sprint, Coach Sewell came over and told me I was pretty fast for a guy my size. He said, "You need to tell your parents that I said you should come out for football." Wow, I was excited. One of the coaches wanted me to play football.

That evening, when my dad came home from working at C. W. Mathews Construction Company, I passed along the message from Coach Sewell. My dad looked at me and said, "You tell that SOB that I just spent $90 for you a new trumpet for high school. Tell him to send me $90 and you can play football." Understood and no argument about his message.

The following day in PE, I approached Coach Sewell and I told him, this is what my dad said to tell you. "You tell that SOB I spent $90 to buy you a new trumpet when you started high school. If he wants you to play football, tell him to send me $90." Coach laughed and said, "Walter, enjoy playing in the band." I really enjoyed all four years playing trumpet in the band at football games and concerts at North Cobb High.

THE FIRST NORTH COBB HIGH SCHOOL MEN'S GOLF TEAM

My years at North Cobb High School from 1958 until graduation in 1962 are filled with many memories. Our class of 1962 was the first class to attend all four years of high school at North Cobb. When I was a Junior, Coach Emory Sewell organized the first North Cobb Golf Team. There were only four of us on the first men's golf team, Bill Hartshorn, Cam Hardigree (whose father was the Golf Professional at O. B. Keller Golf Course in Kennesaw, GA later to become Pinetree Country Club), Dwayne Woods and me.

As for talent, Cam and Bill were the best two players. Dwayne and I were the b-players normally scoring in the mid-40s on nine holes, but with a good round, we could occasionally break into the upper 30s. We played several matches, all played at O. B. Keller Golf Course. I cannot recall how many matches we won, but I'm sure Bill and Cam and good rounds by Dwayne and me helped us win some of the matches.

I realize this is a short story, but it is North Cobb High School history and is also to recognize Coach Emory Sewell for organizing that first men's golf team. The North Cobb Golf Letter in the picture was one of the first four golf letters ever issued at North Cobb. I cherish this letter. In talking to some of the ladies in my class, we seem to recall Coach Sewell tried to organize a ladies golf team too, but couldn't find enough participants.

Many of you Experienced Adults (I don't like the term Senior Citizen) from North Cobb will remember that Coach Sewell also managed the swimming pool at O. B. Keller. It was a huge pool with a very tall Olympic diving board. I'll confess, I went to the top diving board one time and looked down. I quickly turned around and walked back down a ladder to a lower diving board. Ok, I've confessed, fear set in on that high board! One day, Coach Sewell took us on a tour of the pool and showed us a stairway that went down to a hallway where there was a window that you could look out into the pool. Thank you again Coach Sewell for all your accomplishments and your treatment of your students.

LESSONS FROM MY FATHER AND MOTHER

I remember, as a kid, living on Fowler Street and the neighborhood boys and girls would get together and play games. Softball, hide and seek, kick the can, etc. My father would tell me often, "Son, treat 'em all like you want 'em to treat you." He told me this when I started school at Acworth School. Before I began working at Dunn's Supermarket, he would tell me to treat the other employees and customers "like you'd want 'em to treat you." Without a doubt, some of the best advice I received.

I began working at Dunn's in 1957 on Fridays after school and all day Saturday from 8 am until 8 pm. When I was a Junior in high school in 1960, one of the older guys who worked at Dunn's would invite us to go to the Drag Races in Dallas, GA on some Saturdays after work. I told my dad one Saturday that the guys were going to the Drag Races after work. He reached into his overhauls pocket and pulled out a nickle. He said, "Son, if you get in any trouble with the police, use this nickle to call someone to come get you out of jail." He added, "Don't call me cause I ain't coming and don't call your mother because she ain't coming either!" If I ever thought about getting in trouble, I would say to myself, "Who would I call?" I never needed the nickle but, unfortunately, I spent it. Oh how I wish I still had that nickle!

The Saturday before I started working at the Atlanta Post Office on December 1, 1962, my dad took me to Atlanta to buy me a car. He was able to get Fred Gayton, a mechanic in Acworth, to go with us and select a good dependable vehicle. After looking at several vehicles, Fred told my father a 55 Ford Victoria was in great shape mechanically. My dad bought it and I drove it home. My dad and Fred went by a beverage store located across the Chattahooche River from Cobb County. I owed my father $550 dollars for the car, and, every two weeks when I received a paycheck, I would pay him $50. He carried a small notebook in the bib pocket of his overhauls. He would pull it out, open it up, and would deduct $50, then he would show me how much I still owed. When I made my last payment, he asked me if I wanted the notebook. I told him no. Why oh why didn't I take and keep that notebook!

In 1964, I was on the way home to Acworth from the Atlanta Post Office Federal Annex. It was after 10:30 pm and I passed a Wade Ford used car lot on Williams Street. I saw this beautiful 1963½ Fastback Ford Galaxie XL with a 390 engine. I stopped and looked it over and decided it was time for me to upgrade from my 1955 Ford Victoria. After giving it a lot of thought, I told my father what I had seen and that I wanted it. It was a weekend and he told me, "Son, take the money you're gonna spend on that car and buy some property. In fact, there's some property down near Kennesaw that's for sale. I think you can get it for a reasonable price." I told him I didn't want no property, I wanted that Ford. He then said, "Let's go look at that land." We jumped in my car and away we went. The property was out in the woods and we looked it over. No homes or anything was in view. After walking the property for a few minutes, I put my hand on my dad's shoulder and said, "Dad, there ain't ever going to be anything here. This is nothing but woods and probably always will be." I secured a loan from the Atlanta Postal Credit Union and bought the Galaxie XL for just over three thousand dollars. Today, when I drive up I-75 and pass the Barrett Parkway exit, just North of that intersection is the property my dad wanted me to buy. Part of it is Kennesaw College, Chastain Road, and maybe even some of Town Center Mall. I look up to the Heavens and say, "Dad, I'm so stupid for not taking your advice. There's the property you wanted me to buy, but I don't have a clue where that 63 Fastback Ford is today!"

My mother worked at Unique Knitting Mill on the 3 pm until 11 pm shift for many years. She taught me and my sister several valuable lessons. One was about housekeeping that served me well all through life. She would tell me and my sister, "The scissors are in the top left drawer of the sewing machine. If I go to use them and they are not there, I'll know one of you has them. As soon as you finish with them, place them back in the drawer where you got them. That way, we'll always know where they are and we'll never have to clean up after ourselves".

In 1965, during my third week in Military Police School at Fort Gordon, GA, Sgt. Walker (my platoon Sgt.) called me over and said, "Flanagan, I've noticed you keep your s**t straight. Accordingly, I've left you a pass over at CQ and you can use it when you're off duty, but, f**k up one time, and your pass will be canceled!" I never disappointed him. Thank you Mother!

THE TURKEY SHOOT

I began working at Dunn's Supermarket in 1957 when it was located just across the street from Burger's Fruit Stand on South Main Street in Acworth. It was a Saturday in November and the Colonial Bread man was stocking the shelves with his product. Afterward, he told Ronald Abernathy, who was one of the cashiers and loved hunting and fishing, that there was a turkey shoot in progress over across the Little Dam. He asked Ronald if he wanted to go there during his upcoming lunch. Ronald said yes but he had only one shotgun in his car. Ronald asked me if my father had a shotgun the Colonial Bread man could use since we lived just over a mile from where the turkey shoot was being held. A few minutes later, we were off to my parents home. I went inside and told my dad what we were doing. I grabbed my dad's twelve gauge bolt action shotgun for the bread man and a long barrel twelve gauge single shot shotgun that had belonged to my grandfather that I would use. Ronald had the ammunition.

When we arrived at the turkey shoot, we paid one dollar each which entitled us to one shot at a target. I don't remember exactly how far away these targets were, but they were white cardboard squares and had an 'X' drawn across each one. They were also numbered to match the number on the location at the firing line. The object was to get as close to the middle of the 'X' as possible. All those who paid lined up, loaded their shotguns, and prepared to fire. Then came the command, "Ready.......Set.......Fire!

A volunteer then gathered the targets and they examined them to see who had won. I couldn't believe it, but I won. They showed the target and there were only five holes from the pellets in the entire target, but, luckily, one of them was right through the middle of the 'X'. The prize was a live turkey. Ronald took the turkey, put it in his trunk, and we drove by my parents home to return the shotguns and give them the turkey. Then it was back to work for the three of us.

After we arrived at Dunn's, it was an afternoon of harassment for me. Ronald and the bread man said that I only had five holes in my target. I should be ashamed of myself for taking a prize. The story spread to all those who worked at Dunn's. Finally, I developed a come back line. "At least I hit the middle of the target, no one else did." My dad readied the turkey for cooking and my mother prepared it for our Sunday meal. It wasn't our usual Sunday meal of fried chicken, but I was proud of myself for winning this turkey.

HIGH SCHOOL HOME ROOM

Not long ago, I was talking with a classmate about North Cobb High School from 1958 through 1962, the year we graduated. I was a member of the first class to attend North Cobb for all four years. The discussion came around to talking about our home room experiences.

We had individual lockers and, time permitting, I would stop by my locker after getting off the school bus. Then it was time for Home Room when the bell rang. The home room teacher would perform some administrative duties after calling the roll. At that time, the person who was to read the Bible would get it off the teacher's desk. The reading was on a rotating basis and you kept up with the rotation so that you would be prepared when it was your turn.

When it was time for the Bible reading, the person would stand before the class, open the Bible and tell the class the chapter and verses they would be reading. They would read the passage and we would then stand and recite the Lord's Prayer. After the prayer, we would remain standing and recite the Pledge of Allegiance.

One of my classmates would read the same brief passage every time. It never failed. He would cite the chapter and verse and then say, "Jesus wept. Let us pray." The teacher would smile after he did it the first few times. Some classmates would also say along with him, "Jesus wept. Let us pray."

I don't know what they do in high school home room these days with all the political correctness. In fact, I don't know if they still have home rooms. I can truly say that my home room experience never hurt me. "Let us pray."

MR. CANTRELL
WANTS TO SEE YOU
IN HIS OFFICE

One afternoon I was seated at my typewriter in my Typing II class when Mrs. Smith, our teacher, approached my desk and told me that Mr. Steve Cantrell wanted to see me in his office. I asked what for, and she smiled and shrugged her shoulders. Getting up from my chair and making my way out of the classroom, I began to think back on the day. What had I done wrong? Thinking of nothing that would get me an office visit, my mind wandered back over the last few days, but still nothing.

Arriving at the office, I told the lady at the front that Mrs. Smith told me Mr. Cantrell wanted to see me. She said he was out of his office for a minute or so, but go in and have a seat. I went through the door into his office and, having never been there, looked around at the pictures, diplomas, and books on the shelves. About the time I took my seat, Mr. Cantrell came through the door. He asked me if I wanted a Coca Cola. "Yes sir, thank you, I'll take one." He returned in a very short time with my Coke and took his seat. "Mrs. Smith told me you were the best male typist in North Cobb. We are having a District Competition next month and I would like for you to represent us by competing against the males from the other schools." Without hesitation, I told him, "Sure, I would love to do so." He thanked me, told me to hurry and finish my Coke and get back to class.

The day for the competition arrived and, before leaving North Cobb, I selected my manual Royal typewriter from my typing class and loaded it into the school bus. Girls were also competing against each other in typing and shorthand. I don't recall any males from North Cobb competing in shorthand, but I could be wrong. I can't remember where this District meet was held, but I took my typewriter inside and followed instructions as to where to go for the event. About ten to twelve other males were in the room setting up their typewriters and then a lady came in and told us what we would be doing in a very few minutes. It would be a ten minute timed writing with the winner being determined by the most words for minute with the fewest errors.

We were given a short few minutes to read the material after it was placed on our desk face down. I placed the material on a stand beside my typewriter and, 'Ready, Set, Type' and the competition was on. My best ten minute timed writing in Mrs. Smith's class had been ninety words per minute with only two errors. When time was up, we wrote our name and school on the material, and then we handed it to the instructor. We stayed in the room until they returned with the results. I had won the blue ribbon with a timed writing in the upper eighties with two errors.

Mr. Cantrell was there and he congratulated me for my success. I wish I could recall who won the ladies typing and shorthand competitions, but, unfortunately, a search of our North Cobb Annual for that year did not contain those results.

Years later, when I began serving as a Management Arbitration Advocate for the Postal Service, I wished many times I had taken shorthand in high school. Of course, back in those days, males normally didn't take shorthand classes. The typing ability served me well throughout my career with the Postal Service. The picture above is the award I won that day. Thank you Mrs. Smith and Mr. Cantrell.

DENTISTS I HAVE KNOWN AND LOVED?

My first visit to a dentist was in the fifties in Acworth. His name was Dr. Reed and he had an office near Acworth School. I would usually ride my bicycle over to his office. When I had a cavity, he would deaden my gums before the cavity repair. He would hold the syringe containing the novocaine up in front of you and push to cause a stream of the drug to come out of the needle. Then he would say, this is going to sting a bit. He was right and I hated it. This was well before the agent they now use on your gums to deaden the area before giving you the injection. And, today, they never let you see the needle. I reached the point where I would ask Dr. Reed if he could do the filling without me needing the injections. A few times he did and I was so happy not to see the needle and feel the stinging of my gums.

Later in life, I would see Dr. Zim Choate in Cartersville, GA. I was still living in Acworth with my parents and was working at the Atlanta Post Office. One afternoon, I had an appointment and it was for a root canal. They called me back and I was treated to several injections to deaden my gums around the area. When the drug took effect, Dr. Zim performed the root canal. About an hour later, I was so happy to leave the office. There was a drive through beer store nearby, so I drove through and purchased a large can of Papst Blue Ribbon. Pulling over under some shade trees, I popped the top and brought the can up to my deadened mouth. I turned the can up and the beer began pouring out of my mouth. I had so much deadening, I couldn't completely close my mouth. Consequently, most of beer ran out of my mouth and down all over my shirt. I dropped the rest of the beer in a nearby trash can and drove back to Acworth.

In the late nineties, I needed some gum surgery so I was referred to Dr. O'Brien in Macon, GA. After my injections were accomplished and a few minutes passed, Dr. O'Brien came in to begin the procedure. Well, about halfway through the surgery, Dr. O'Brien told me she was giving me a break for a few minutes. I told her something she never forgot. I said, "Dr., if you were doing to animals in here what you're doing to me, there would be people outside carrying protest signs." She laughed and later returned to finish her work. Thereafter, for my next couple of visits to her office for teeth cleaning, she comes in after the technician finishes the cleaning, says hello, and looks out the window. "Nobody out there carrying signs Walter" she says, smiling!

RED RUN

O n December 1, 1962, I walked into the Atlanta Post Office Federal Annex as a Part-Time Flexible Distribution Clerk. I was eighteen years old by exactly two months. During orientation, I was assigned a state scheme and, after a couple of hours, we were taken out to the workroom floor. Those who had a state scheme were taken to the Second Floor where parcel post going to Georgia, North and South Carolina arrived on a belt in large sacks from downstairs. The large bags of parcel post were brought over by trucks from the Terminal Station after arrival by train. Our job was to sort the parcels by city by state, place the parcels back in number one sacks, and drop them down a chute where they would be moved by belt to the back dock for loading on trucks and dispatched for delivery. Didn't mean to bore you with details, but you were on your feet all day. I worked ten hours my first day, then twelve hour days every day thereafter through December 23. My hours were from 2 pm in the afternoon until 2:30 am.

A few days before Christmas, one of my fellow employees named Woody, a big man, came over to me and told me to follow him. He had a red baseball cap on at the time. We went into a small room just off the workroom floor and he asked me if I knew how to use a pistol. I had fired them before so I told him I did. He told me to take a pistol out of the drawer, load it, then place a holster on my belt and insert the pistol in the holster. I asked him what were we doing, and he explained we were going on a 'red run'. He told me we were going over to the Terminal Station to retrieve registered mail from a Railway Post Office (RPO). They would know him by the red hat and the fact he had made these runs previously.

I followed him to the elevator and we rode downstairs to the basement of the Federal Annex. We departed the elevator and walked several yards to a tunnel. That tunnel went under Spring Street and came out track level at the Terminal Station. We then kept walking over to a passenger like rail car that was a Railway Post Office (RPO). When Woody walked up, one of the clerks inside the car retrieved a number two sack that had a lock on it. The lock had a number on it that could be seen through a plastic cover. Woody checked the number and then signed for receipt of the mail sack. We then started walking back toward the tunnel. Woody stopped after a few steps and told me something I will never forget. He said, "If anybody tries to take this bag of mail from me, you shoot them. This mail is registered mail and worth a lot of money." I promised I would.

Talk about looking around as we walked over to the tunnel, through the tunnel to the basement, then up the elevator to the Registered Mail Cage on the First Floor, I watched everything. When we arrived at the Registered Section, a man inside the cage took the bag of mail, checked the number on the lock, then signed for the mail. Our mission was successful. We took the elevator up to the Second Floor and turned in our weapons. Woody thanked me for accompanying him on the Red Run. He told me he selected me because I was a big guy over six foot tall and weighed over two hundred pounds. I made several other Red Runs with him over the coming months, but I'll never forget my first one!

MY TRIUMPH BONNEVILLE

RIDING MY TRIUMPH BONNEVILLE FOR THE FIRST TIME

I was working at the Atlanta Post Office and, one day in mid-1964, a Tour Superintendent approached and asked if I would be interested in a detail to the Sears & Roebuck Detached Postal Unit on Ponce de Leon in Atlanta. He told me they presorted the parcels mailed by Sears prior to them being hauled by trucks over to the Parcel Post Annex. I had qualified on the Georgia Scheme so I could start tomorrow if I wished to do so. Oh, and the great thing about this detail was the hours, 9 am to 5:30 pm with off days of Saturdays and Sundays. My current shift at the Federal Annex was from 2 pm to 10:30 pm with rotating off days so I couldn't say YES fast enough.

In 1966, one of the guys I worked with at Sears told me he had a friend who had a 1965 Triumph Bonneville motorcycle for sale. He rode a Harley Davidson and it looked like fun, so I went with him after work one day to see the Triumph. The guy who was selling it was a barber in a shop across the street from the Varsity in Atlanta. He parked his motorcycle at the Varsity while he worked. It was beautiful with a gold and white gas tank and I decided to buy it. We worked out a deal and made arrangements for me to pick it up the next day. Since I had never ridden a motorcycle before, I asked a couple of guys in Acworth who did ride if they would go with me to Atlanta from Acworth and ride the Triumph back to my home. Neither could go due to work schedules, so I got a friend I had worked with at Dunn's Supermarket to go with me and drive my car back and I would ride the motorcycle.

Upon our arrival in the Varsity parking lot, the seller came over and showed me how to operate the Triumph. He demonstrated how to start it, how to change gears, the brakes and the gas which was located on the right handlebar grip. I got on the cycle, started it, held the clutch in, pushed it down into first gear and gently gave it gas. I went out of the Varsity parking lot and onto the street, coasted down to the ramp to the expressway, turned onto the ramp, gave it some gas and blended into the traffic heading home. I changed the gears and my top speed most of the way home was fifty miles per hour. I was so happy to get my new motorcycle home. Thinking back on this experience, today, at my age, I wouldn't ride that Triumph from the Varsity in Atlanta to Acworth if you gave it to me! Thank you Lord for giving me a safe trip home on that day!

THE GOODYEAR BLIMP

In the summer of 1978, I was working in Columbia, SC on a detail to a U. S. Postal Service Sectional Center Human Resources Manager assignment. The HR Manager was retiring and they needed someone to fill the assignment temporarily until it could be filled permanently. I was a Labor Relations Representative in Atlanta and had a goal of obtaining a HR Manager assignment. In acceptance of the detail, it was understood that I could not apply for the job, but it would gain me experience in an assignment like one I wanted on a permanent basis.

It was a learning assignment and I met some wonderful people. The Sectional Center Manager was a very good manager and, low did I know at the time, but our paths would cross again in the early 2000s as he and the guy who was selected to permanently fill the HR position and I all had recreational vehicles. Charlie reserved three recreational vehicle spaces at the Fairgrounds in Columbia, SC and game tickets to attend the Georgia Bulldog/South Carolina Gamecock football game. We could walk over to the stadium from the Fairgrounds. We would, through the following years, meet and play golf and attend several more GA/SC football games. Unfortunately, Charlie passed away in March of 2017.

One Friday in 1978, I was leaving Columbia at about one pm for the four plus hour drive to my apartment in Marietta and decided I wanted a cold beer. I stopped at a service station near the I-20 entrance, went inside and purchased a cold beer and, while I filled my car with gas, I consumed the beer I had wrapped in a napkin. I then threw the empty can in a trash container, and away I went.

As I was driving through Augusta, GA, the urge to download some beer hit me. I didn't want to waste a lot of time getting off I-20 and stopping at a fast food restaurant to use their restroom. Just above Augusta was an exit with nothing on either side of the road. Well, I was really under pressure to go by that time, so, at the top of the exit, I pulled over into a small area, opened the door of my car, got out, and unzipped. About that time I heard an engine overhead and looked up to see the Goodyear Blimp. Actually, it came right over me and was flying low. I could not stop downloading the beer, so I looked up and waved. Luckily, I never learned of any 'film at eleven' from the blimp on the local television news reports that evening!

SHI**ING IN HIGH COTTON

Where the Hell is Shreveport?

After my divorce in 1977 (no children), I moved into an apartment complex in Marietta, GA. Post Ridge Apartments was located just over a mile East of the Big Chicken on Roswell Road. We had two swimming pools, six tennis courts, and a pub. A group would gather on Friday nights at the pub, have a few drinks, then it was off to one of the Atlanta area Discos. A lady in that group named Deanna was also known as the 'Social Director'. Late Sunday afternoons after tennis, we would gather at the pub and bring a covered dish. If there was a good concert in the area, she would organize a group to attend the event. A great singles complex, but, little did I know, I would be leaving Post Ridge in 1978.

There was a Sectional Center Human Resources Manager assignment posted for Shreveport, Louisiana. It was the same level as the detail assignment I held in Columbia, SC so I applied. A few weeks later, interviews were held and, a week or so afterward, I received a call from the Sectional Center Manager informing me that I was the successful applicant. Then it was off to Shreveport for a house hunting trip. I found a nice new apartment complex across the street from Louisiana State University, Shreveport. To reach the complex, you had to drive on a paved road through about a one hundred yard wide cotton field. The apartment complex had one swimming pool and one tennis court. I moved there in November of 1978.

Several of the guys who lived there worked on oil drilling facilities and would be away for several days at a time. I also met a guy who liked to play tennis, so, weather permitting, we played tennis on the weekends and, at times, after work. One Saturday I had a great idea and I asked him to help me. It was shorts weather and the cotton had not been picked/gathered. I got between two of the rows of tall cotton, pulled down my shorts and underwear, squatted, and had him snap a picture. You couldn't see anything other than me squatting with cotton all around me, so, when the pictures came back from developing, I took that one and mailed it to my mother. I told her in my letter that I was 'Shi**ing In High Cotton' in Shreveport'. A few days later, I called her and asked what she thought of my picture. She said, "Aren't you ashamed of yourself?" Not the first time I'd heard that from her. We laughed and she caught me up with the latest news from Acworth.

GOLF LESSONS IN BIRMINGHAM, ALABAMA

I was on a detail to the Birmingham Division Human Resources Manager assignment back in 1987 while my friend Jerry Selmon was at National Negotiations. The Division Manager was a good golfer and was winning my per diem just about every time we played. This had to stop. I went to a nearby driving range one day at lunchtime and they had a man who gave lessons. I told him that I was interested in a thirty minute lesson, and could he do it while I was on my lunch break. "Yes sir", he said.

Let me describe this older gentleman. He was late-sixties, under six feet tall, and probably weighed just over two hundred pounds I guessed. He wore a large brim straw hat with a green visor in the front brim of the hat. He introduced himself and told me how long he had been playing. Then, because I guess I looked a bit apprehensive, he said, "Walter, see that large 150 yard marker down the range? Well, I'm going to take my driver and hit one right over the 150 yard marker." He made a nice swing and the ball sailed right over the 150 yard marker. "Now, he said, just to show you that wasn't luck, I'll hit another one over the 150 yard marker." Another nice swing and the ball again went over the 150 yard marker on about the same line as his first shot. He then said, "Walter, do I have your attention now?" I told him "Bud, you're looking at Dumbo the Elephant, I'm all ears"!

I came back to the driving range a few days later after work and took another lesson. These two lessons helped me hit the ball straighter as I learned I had a grip problem. I did take some money from the Division Manager, but, on our last round of golf prior to my return to my Southern Region Labor Relations assignment in Memphis, TN., he won it back!

CORNELL STORIES

YOU DON'T KNOW HOW
TO DO WHAT?

In 1995, I was fortunate to have an opportunity to attend Cornell University for a two week Advanced Human Resources Managers course. At the time, I was a District Human Resources Manager with the South Georgia District of the United States Postal Service. Orientation for the course would be on a Sunday afternoon beginning at 2 pm, so I had to fly up on Saturday to assure I would be there for this event. I rented a car for the two weeks and drove to the French Quarter Inn where we would be staying for the first week. The Statler Hotel on campus was full and could not accommodate our class for the first week. We would move there for the second week of classes.

I arrived at the French Quarter Inn on Saturday afternoon after four pm and checked in. The lady at the front desk told me that a Hospitality Suite had been set up for those of us attending the course. I went to my room, unpacked and then made my way to the Hospitality Suite. I was the only one there, so I opened a beer and had a snack as all I had on the flight from Atlanta was peanuts. Golf was on the television, so I watched and snacked and decided to have another beer.

About half way through that second beer, a lady walked in and I introduced myself. She was also attending the course. She was a blonde, about thirty, and she told me she was an attorney for a record company. She looked around the room and asked if there was any vodka. I told her all I found was beer and wine, but I too liked vodka and maybe we could get some at a liquor store nearby as I had a rental car. We decided to go to the front desk and inquire as to the location of a liquor store. The lady gave us directions and out the front door we went.

As we approached the car, I took out my keys and said, "I've had a couple of beers so here's the keys, you drive." She said, "I don't know how to drive a car." I said, "You don't know how to do what?" She explained that she had lived in or near New York City all her life and that you don't want a car in New York City. She also said that, when on vacation, she always rode with friends or took public transportation. Wow! I could not imagine not knowing how to drive or not owning a car. So began my two weeks at Cornell University!

STEVE ALLEN'S SON

O ur last evening at Cornell was a Thursday so we had a celebration. Friday would be a travel day to return home. The evening began with happy hour, then, we boarded a bus and rode to a nice restaurant for dinner. A couple of guys in the course and I had been drinking adult beverages and telling stories of our human resources experiences. It was an evening to kick back and enjoy after working our way through this course.

Steve Allen's son was to provide the entertainment for the evening. One of the professors introduced him, and Steve's son told us what he would be doing after we had dinner. He then began telling us about his father. I had watched the Steve Allen Show on television in the late 50s, early 60s and enjoyed the 'Man on the Street' interviews with Tom Poston, Louie Nye and Don Knotts.

While Steve's son was talking about his father, he reached up and tugged on his hair and said, "My father and Burt Reynolds have something in common. Do you know what it is?" I said loudly, "Yea, neither is currently married to Loni Anderson!" (Burt and Loni had divorced a year or so earlier as I recall.) He laughed loudly, somewhat similar to his dad's great laugh. After a few minutes, he told us he would return after our meal.

When we finished our meal, he returned and came over to my table. He told me that, while we were eating, he called his father and told him what I had said. He said his father broke up with laughter. I thanked him for telling me and told him I would love to have heard his dad laugh. Steve Allen provided many laughs for me during his years on television, and I'm happy to know I was able to pay him back with one good laugh!

BEST $20 DOLLAR GOLF COURSE I EVER PLAYED

In the summer of 2000, we were on our retirement trip in our motor home and working our way down the West Coast. I called ahead and tried to get a tee time at Torrey Pines Golf Course. Nothing during the dates we would be nearby. When we arrived in the San Diego area, we found a nice motor home park and stayed a few days. We tow a Jeep Wrangler, so we unhooked and toured the area.

I told my wife we need to go to Torrey Pines and get hats or shirts or something in addition to looking over the courses. It's in a beautiful location setting on some high cliffs overlooking the Pacific Ocean. We were in the clubhouse purchasing some shirts and hats and I started a conversation with a guy behind the counter. I told him I had called and tried to get a tee time two weeks ago and could get nothing in the time we planned to be in the area. He asked did I care what time I played. I said I'd play at night if he would hold the flashlight. He laughed and told me that, in a few minutes a booth would open out on the patio and they would be selling tee times starting at 4 pm. Your fee will be $20 since you're from out of state. Locals pay only $10. He said we would not get eighteen holes in due to darkness. He then saw a guy walk by the door heading for the booth on the patio and told me to go get behind him. I did and was fortunate enough to get the second tee time at 4:10 pm on the North Course.

We were excited as we drove back to our motor home and loaded our clubs into the Jeep. When we teed off on the first hole, it ran out toward the cliffs and the ocean. What a beautiful place. So much scenery on each of the fourteen holes we were able to play before dark. Absolutely, positively, and without a doubt, the BEST $20 golf course I've ever played!

ROCKY MOUNTAIN SPOTTED FEVER

I was playing golf in late May, 2017 at a nearby golf course. Our seniors group played at this course every Tuesday and Thursday. The course has some holes surrounded by homes and several with woods on one or both sides of the fairway. Hole number fourteen had woods on both sides along with two lakes. You had to carry one lake on your tee shot and another lake on your approach to the green. One of our foursome hit a ball into the woods to the right and we went in to look for it. After coming out of the woods, I felt a tick on the back of my leg. One of the other players told me to look down because blood was coming down from a tick bite just below my right knee. I pulled the tick out and crushed him on the cart path. I also pulled off the one on the back of my left leg. Our home is on two wooded acres so I've had many bites and encounters with ticks crawling on me. Never had any problems.

In the first week of June, I began to get dizzy. My doctor had recently changed a medication and the information noted that it may cause slight dizziness. That must be what it was. To make a long story short, in the early am of Saturday morning, June 10, I got out of bed to use the restroom. I was extremely dizzy and tried to hold on to the foot of the bed, but instead, I fell to the floor. My wife woke to find me on the floor and unable to get myself up to my feet. I used to see that commercial where they say, "Help, I've fallen and I can't get up", and smile a little, but I don't anymore. Elaine quickly called 911 and they arrived within a very few minutes. They loaded me onto a stretcher and transported me to Navicent Health Hospital in Macon.

They took me upstairs to the Intensive Care Unit where I was to remain for the next five days. I've never been so sick. A crew of physicians were treating me and, late on day three or early on day four, they told me I had Rocky Mountain Spotted Fever and they were giving me antibiotics via IV. I began feeling better and, at the end of day five, they released me. I was still dizzy but could move around without a walker. It was great to get home and sleep in my own bed.

On a follow up visit, one of the doctors told me they would have diagnosed the problem sooner if I had been a fisherman or hunter. Guess they figured I was a golfer who always stayed in the fairway. After I began playing golf again with the seniors group, I sprayed down heavily with Deep Woods Off with deet. I also told every one of them what I had endured and urged them to spray. I never entered the woods again to look for my ball or one of theirs. They are making new golf balls everyday, so I will NOT go after one if I hit it into the woods!

MOTHER-IN-LAW'S 90ᵀᴴ BIRTHDAY

January of 2018 and my wife Elaine's mother is about to turn ninety. There's a party for her at one of her sister's homes and she will be learning of the surprise gift on the Sunday before her birthday. Many friends from her hometown and from her church were at the party that Sunday afternoon.

After all guests had been served a slice of the birthday cake and other treats, it was time to reveal the surprise gift. Elaine (my wife) came out onto the screened porch wearing a huge Mexican sombrero and presented her mother with a ticket for a four day cruise to Cozemel, Mexico. It would be aboard the Brilliance of the Seas and would sail out of Tampa, FL on Thursday following the Sunday party. She would be joined on the cruise by approximately thirty family members and friends.

The cruise was fun and, of course, there was more than ample food and drink. On Friday night, after our evening meal, the servers brought a beautiful birthday cake and everyone sang Happy Birthday. While we were eating the delicious cake, we heard the servers singing Happy Birthday on the other side of the large dining room. We said, "Hey, someone has the same birthday as you." Several minutes passed and one of the servers came over to Elaine's mother, tapped her on the shoulder and said, "You have some catching up to do. That lady on the other side of the dining room is 100 today." We asked him to tell her Happy Birthday from all of us.

Leaving the dining room, the birthday ladies met and had a wonderful conversation. Neither of them was on a walker, used a cane or was on oxygen. Both were blessed with good health. I'm so glad they were able to meet on that evening, truly one of the highlights of this cruise.

WHAT IF . . . . ?

Sitting on the sofa one afternoon after reading through the day's mail, the dog lying nearby on the sofa sleeping, I kicked back the recliner and began thinking, 'what if?'. You've done it I'm sure in some quiet moments of reflection. You think back over your life and wonder what would have happened 'if'. Below are some of my 'what if' thoughts.

What if I hadn't gone with my cousin and applied to take the Post Office Department Examination while I was a senior in high school? Not one of the greatest students in high school, I really didn't know what I wanted to do after graduation. I knew that in October, when I turned eighteen, I intended to apply for a job at Lockheed. Until then, I would work full time for Dunn's Supermarket.

What if I had joined the Air Force when a high school friend, Leon Thompson, and I went to Marietta to talk with an Air Force Recruiter. We had graduated from high school and talked about joining together. I had been a member of the Camera Club in my last two years of high school. Coach Sewell was the leader of the Camera Club and I was interested in taking good pictures. At that time, you had a roll of film in your camera and you snapped the pictures. You would then take the roll of film to a drug store and wait a few days until they were developed. My mother found Jack Rabbit Photo located in Chattanooga, TN. We would mail our rolls of film to them and they would process it and return it in a few days. It was always an exciting time when your pictures were delivered in the mail. Later, when Town and Country Shopping Center opened on Roswell Road in Marietta, there was a round building in the parking lot where you could drop your film off and the pictures would be ready in one hour. After talking with the Air Force Recruiter and telling him I wanted to be a photographer, he said he could not guarantee me that's what I would be assigned if I joined. Leon was told the same thing about his choice. We didn't join.

The day I turned eighteen, my mother drove me to Marietta to sign up for the draft and to register to vote. On our way back to Acworth, she drove by McLaurin Manufacturing Company where my friend Bobby Odom worked. I went in and completed an application. The lady asked me to wait for a minute while she took my application back to a manager. A couple of minutes later, he came out and asked if I could go to work that afternoon at 2 pm. I told him I didn't have a car. He said a man who was a Supervisor lived in Acworth and he would call him to give me a ride to and from work. His name was Donald Willis and he lived in Grizzletown. He would pick me up at Harrellson's Store on Highway 41 at 1:30 pm. I told him I would need to call my boss, Ralph Dunn, at the Supermarket and see if I needed to give him a notice. Ralph told me if I was making more money, take the job. I did and worked there for two months before being called to work at the Atlanta Post Office. What if my Mother had not driven by McLaurin that October 1, 1962 morning?

About five years into my Post Office career, I applied for a Personnel Assistant assignment for which I was not selected. What if I had not taken some advice from a union steward to request an appointment with the Personnel Manager to learn what I could do to become qualified for any future Personnel Assistant assignment? I called and made an appointment and Arthur Griggs, the Union Steward, went with me to talk to the Personnel Manager. He told me they needed people on detail from time to time and would schedule me for a typing examination. A week or so later, I got a call scheduling me for the exam. I had been practicing on my manual typewriter at home in anticipation of the event. Luckily, I typed 56 words per minute with no errors in a ten minute timed writing. When I arrived back at the Parcel Post Annex, the Tour Superintendent saw me and asked what in the Hell did I do down there, they want me to call and be down there tomorrow morning on a detail. That was my last day at the Parcel Post Annex.

What if I had not seen my wife's roommate at a pub in our apartment complex after they had moved out and asked her for Elaine's phone number? What if she had declined my request for a date? What if, after dating a few years, including a long distance relationship, she had not accepted my proposal one evening at the Coach & Six Restaurant in Atlanta?

Well, these were just a few examples of my 'what ifs'. I could give many more about my thirty-seven year plus Postal Service career and seventy-five years of life. I think it's only natural to wonder about events in your life, but, in looking back, I believe that the Good Lord provided guidance throughout my life. I am so blessed, and I thank God in my daily prayers!

REMEMBERING
MR. BLOCKER

In my first book, my last story was about Mr. Blocker. I will end this book with another story about Mr. Blocker. For those who have not read my previous book, he was my seventh grade teacher at Acworth School. He taught a Health class and, the first day, he told us something I never forgot. He said, "When I enter this room, you will immediately sit up, shut up, and pay attention." We did! He attended our fifty year class reunion and, as emcee, I introduced him and told the story. My classmates loved it.

The next time I saw him was at the funeral of Coach Mathews, a longtime coach at Acworth School and, later, North Cobb High. Upon entering the church, I saw Mr. Blocker talking to another

Acworth friend. I walked up and shook his hand and thanked him for coming to our reunion. He told me he had read my story about Growing up in Acworth in the fifties in the Acworth Magazine, and found no 'dangling participles'. He also said I should write more stories. My sister had been urging me for months to write a book. I told him if I did write a book, he would get one of the first copies.

A month or so later, he send me a letter containing two articles about self-publishing. I sent him a reply, told him I had several stories drafted and appreciated the information. In the Fall of 2014, I had my first book published and, as promised, I sent him a copy and one of the t-shirts I had printed with the logo, 'A GOOD OLD BOY FROM ACWORTH'. In early December of 2014, I scheduled a book signing at the Center Street Tavern in Acworth. Many friends came by and received signed copies of my book. About an hour into the event, one of my friends said, "Look who's coming through the front door." It was Mr. Blocker and he had on the t-shirt I had sent him. I was blown away by his appearance, especially wearing the t-shirt. Several former students spoke with him and had their pictures taken with him. A friend took the above picture of several people holding a copy of my book. Mr. Blocker is on the left. What a great day it was!

In early 2017, Mr. Blocker sent me another letter about different parts of speech, this time, gerunds. He had enjoyed the story in my previous book about him and our conversation about 'dangling participles'. At the end of the letter, he told me that his cancer had returned. He wrote, "Ben said the injections would cause hot flashes, and he was right." I immediately wrote him back and told him he was in my prayers and, hopefully, he would overcome cancer again. Sadly, he passed away in the summer of 2017. I could not attend the funeral as I was recovering from Rocky Mountain spotted fever, thanks to the wrong tick biting me at a local golf course. A great man who helped me and many others throughout his career. We miss you Mr. Blocker!